To the memory of my father, Edward W. Carter

Surrender • 1990

ILLUMINATIONS

WILLIAM CARTER

EDITIONS ONE · SAN FRANCISCO

Acknowledgements

A fifteen-year (and running) project such as this is fed by many tributaries. Thanks to all, including those I've forgotten to mention.

Those who have appreciated and supported the value of my photography of the nude from an early stage include my wife, Ulla; friends Peter Jones and Roger Lipsey of New York, and Weston Naef of Los Angeles, all of whom offered helpful guidance in the preparation of this book; a number of long-faithful dealers including Mary Jean Place of Palo Alto, Lorraine Davis of Zurich, Celina Lunsford of Frankfurt, Wolfgang Kleine of Worpswede/Bremen, Giovanna Chiti of Milan, Nikki Akehurst of London, and Linda Moore of Mill Valley; and many collectors, particularly Mr. & Mrs. Herman De Kesel of Palo Alto and Mr. & Mrs. Marco Pfeifer of Zurich.

Of those involved professionally in the making of *Illuminations*, heartfelt thanks first and foremost to my numerous models – co-creators of these images. To my friend, and a wonderful designer – Sydney King. And to a publisher in all ways sensitive and elegant – Ron Fouts of Custom & Limited Editions.

© William Carter 1996

Book Design: Sydney King ARCA, FRSA King Design Associates International, London

Published by EDITIONS ONE, 41 Sutter Street # 1634 San Francisco, California 94104

ISBN 1-881529-14-2 Paperback

ISBN 1-881529-15-0 Clothbound

Library of Congress Catalog Card Number: 96-085564

Typesetting by DL Graphics Ltd, London

Printed and bound in Italy

Contents

'By That Light all this is illumined'

UPANISHADS

Foreword

There was a time when the words 'humanism' and 'photography' were almost synonymous. Photography earned its place among the fine arts a century ago in large part because even its detractors were persuaded that a photograph could advance traditional humanistic values through the poetic sensibilities of the photographer when combined with an affecting subject.

William Carter is a dedicated humanist. He brings a deep respect for the photographic image to express, in visual language, meanings that until the mid-twentieth century were fundamental to all art. Carter's photographs and words persist in addressing the paramount issues of beauty and mastery, as well as corollaries of philosophy, music, poetry and the human spiritual instinct. He is a man of great faith in the potential for human beings to manifest profound themes, and he has a great respect for the redemptive power of art, and the healing role beauty plays in everyday life. However, 'beauty' means different things to different people. To Simone Weil 'Beauty is the supreme mystery of this world. It is a gleam which attracts the attention and yet does nothing to hold it. Beauty always promises but never gives anything; it stimulates hunger but has no nourishment for the part of the soul which looks in this world for sustenance.' By direct contrast D.H. Lawrence remarked that 'Beauty is not a snare, nor is it skin deep…and if you don't judge by appearances, that is, if you can't trust the impression which things make on you, you are a fool.' Carter's photographs of the human figure test both of these assertions. Although he did not intend them as such, his nudes are a visual answer to the eternal debate between form versus content in art.

Carter has chosen models whose forms and details stand for different varieties of beauty in the human form. Some represent a classical Greek standard, while others suggest the love of abundant flesh typified by the Baroque artists. Carter invites us to judge him and his subjects by the impressions their surface appearances make. He also invites us, through the language of photography, to accept Simone Weil's belief that beauty is, indeed, the supreme mystery of the world; but he challenges her proposition that it is a sterile and nutrionless entity by giving us figures and forms full of an ethical spirit.

To fully comprehend Carter's art, one must also see the other side of his visual personality – his body of documentary and journalistic photography devoted to such subjects as the jazz musicians of New Orleans and the tribal people of Kurdistan. In these, another kind of humanism is evident: action is the vehicle for expressing human potential, and beauty is not the prime emotive force. Why, after a determined search for the nature of such occupations, did Carter decide to pursue its antithesis, the human figure as a collection of abstract lines and forms?

The answer lies in the example of Far Eastern art where tradition, and not innovation, is the chief priority. In his photographs of the human figure Carter is traversing well-established terrain where there is little opportunity to discover new solutions to pose, gesture, expression, lighting, viewpoint, camera angle, or perspective. He is destined to skillfully reinvent solutions for the nude photograph, since most of the variations, combinations and permutations of the elements within the photographer's control have already been tested.

This is not to say there is no room for originality in photographs of the nude – just that it is difficult to achieve. The originality in the present collection resides in the *attitude* Carter brings to the relationship between the model and the photographer. Typically, this has been that of dominant photographer and submissive model. Carter reverses these roles. He shows great respect for his models by the time and talent he devotes to shaping his compositions, and by scrupulous avoidance of the visual codes for erotic involvement. His gaze is neither of voyeur, nor misogynist, nor pornographer, but rather that of the poet adoring his subject with care and tenderness. Humility, not hubris, is the guiding sensibility.

Moreover, we see Carter's attitude as one of submission to the model and to the compositional and physiognomic problems each individual brings to the picture-taking opportunity. We see his role as one of receiving and complementing a vocabulary of forms, not as someone being momentarily in control of the body of another human being. Carter's figure studies are like the art of a scribe who works with a lexicon of canonical words established by higher authority. He is responsible for creating their present manifestation as beautifully and legibly as his materials allow.

WESTON NAEF
Curator of Photographs, J. Paul Getty Museum

Light and Sight

'*Who am I?*' Everyone asks this at some point, in some way. The question hit me with special force in 1976.

Although I didn't yet know it, I was on the verge of a spiritual upheaval which would result, among other things, in the photographs reproduced in this book.

With hindsight I can see that this 'Who am I?' had always been there, teasing at the edges, gnawing at the foundations, motivating from regions beyond awareness. It's now evident to me that my lifelong interest in the arts sprang from a need for self-discovery. This is, of course, a need that never ends, in the sense that life is constantly unfolding, with plenty of snares and revelations. Yet there are those who know who they are. A precious few have the ability to spur that self-knowledge in others.

I had the good fortune to know such a one from 1976 until his death in 1982.

He used to say that you can line up as many zeros as you want: they still amount to nothing until you put that all important 'One' in front of them. The One is at the core of our being. 'Know thyself': Socrates' dictum remains as pivotal in the West as in the East. In a hundred fresh guises, man seeks himself.

Each of us travels the journey anew. My six years of concentrated self-pursuit were many-sided and intense. They came following a difficult time, and in many ways I led the life of a monk, living in one room, meditating reguarly and deeply, travelling to India, getting to know many fellow-seekers, imbibing the teachings of many lineages.

Then, as unexpectedly as I had been swept into that period of my life, in 1982 I was ejected from it. Attempts to continue formal meditation proved so unrewarding that I mostly gave them up. Inexorably, my 'spiritual' living space was

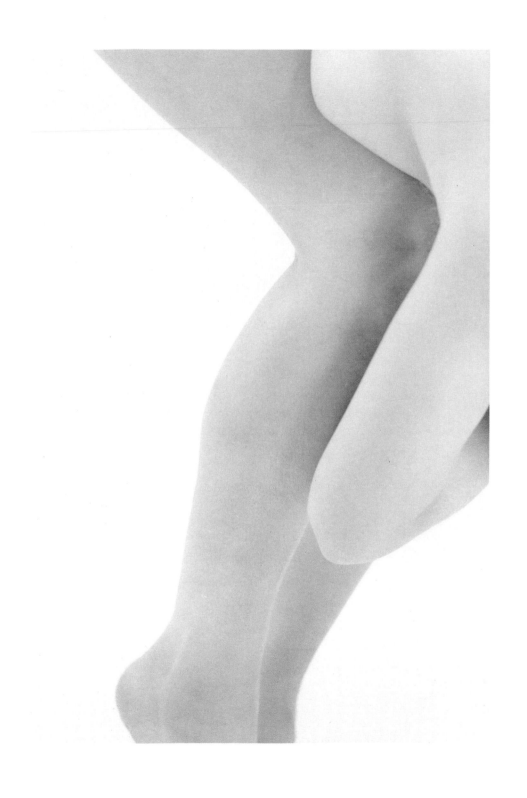

Ripples • 1993

transformed into a photographic studio. I was astonished to find myself doing something I'd never envisioned – least of all in my quasi-monastic mode – photographing nudes. Why, following six years of inward burrowing, should these bright forms suddenly appear in my lenses? Why, after India, *these* images, reminiscent not only of early twentieth century modernism but of its roots: Renaissance Italy and fifth century Athens?

Perhaps the classical is simply too embedded in our institutions, and in ourselves, at levels deeper than language or awareness, to be denied.

And something else:

Moving towards psychic health involves exorcising the less savory elements of our inheritance. Shucking off old restraints leaves our minds and bodies free, untrammeled, naked in the sunshine – like the proud gods of Attica.

Fourteen years later, with the nudes project drawing to an end (or deep pause), I still marvel at the abruptness with which it began. Was this a kind of *koan:* a mind-buster, meant to force one to stop hanging on, even to 'spiritual' life, a going beyond compartments and formulas, including that ancient split between body and spirit?

These themes are explored, in one way or another, in the pages that follow. Assembling *Illuminations* has seemed another work-to-learn assignment from that timeless taskmaster with a billion names, to whom one bows.

Framing Infinity

The curved surface of the lens catches the scattered light, reaching it from all around, then willfully bends the rays to form sharp images at the film plane (retina).

This is the first imposition.

At the film plane the circular image cast by the lens is trimmed to four straight edges.

This is the second imposition.

The photographer has a series of additional choices – film, contrast, image selection, print size, cropping, mode of presentation, etc.

But his most arrogant imposition is to cut a particular slice through space-time with his little shutter button.

The filters of our perceptual mechanism – in the eye itself, all along the optic nerve, in the occipital lobe, and in the centers of learning and judging – impose a series of constrictions on nature, enabling us to comprehend it.

Pure photography imposes no values other than those resident in the photographer's own being.

The camera as third eye: gateway between the inner and the outer.

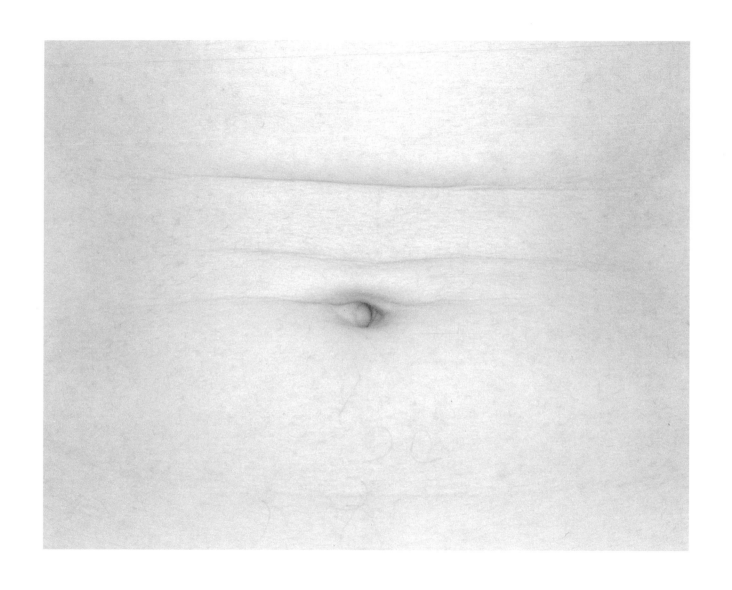

Oneness • 1991

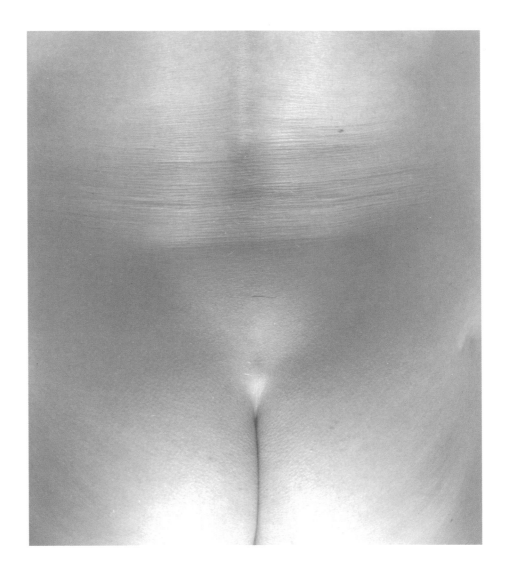

Pond • 1989

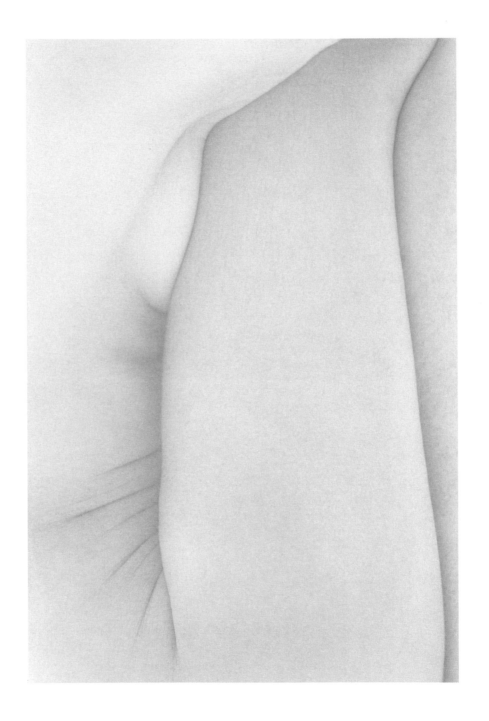

Drawing • 1993

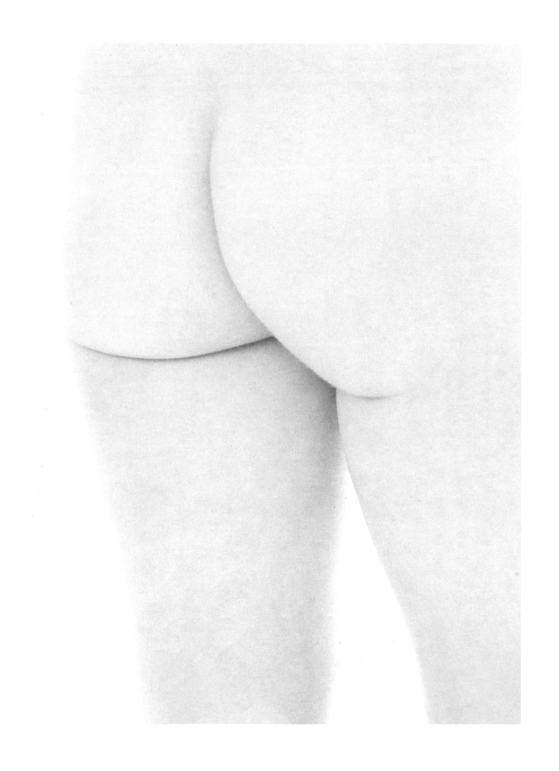

Sketch • 1988

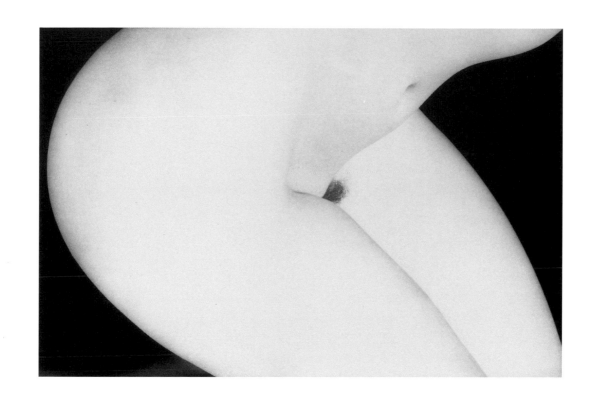

Japanese • 1984

Egg • 1989

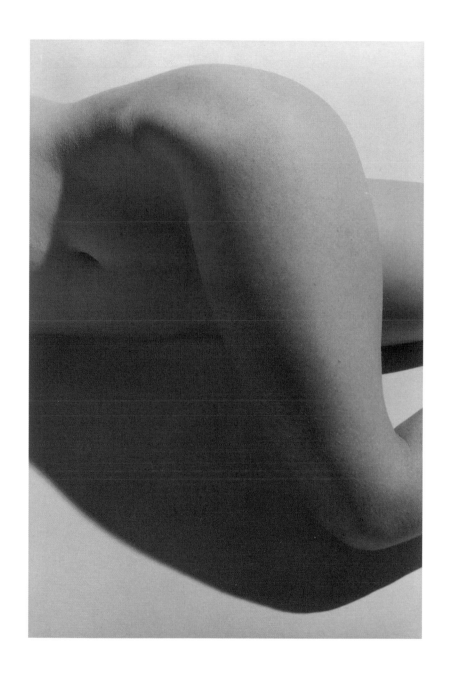

Trace • 1983

Transition • 1992

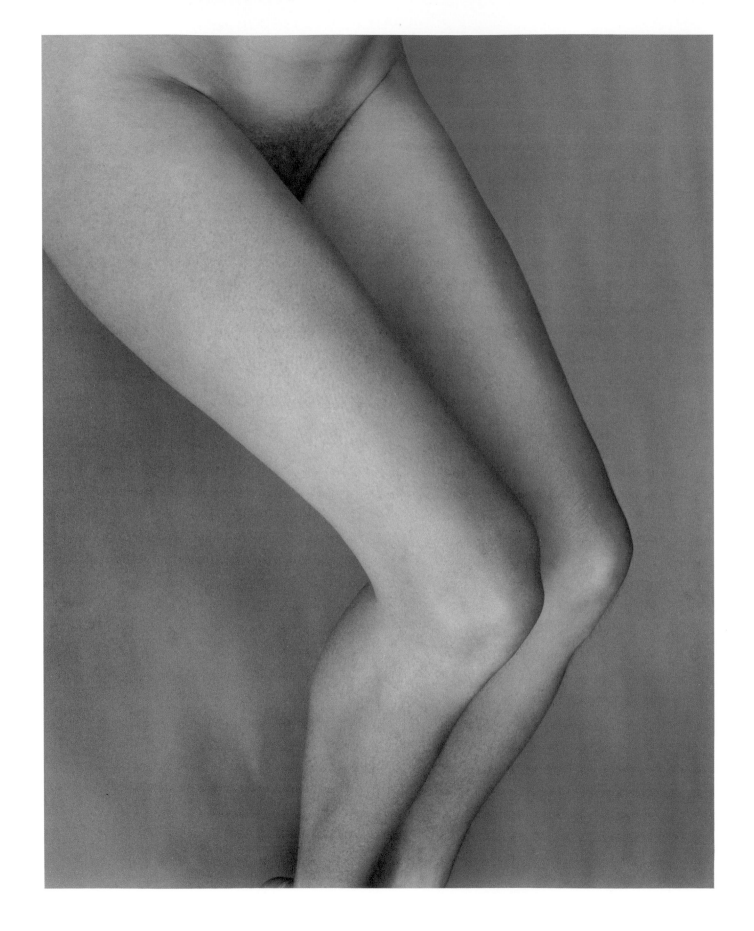

Suspense • 1991

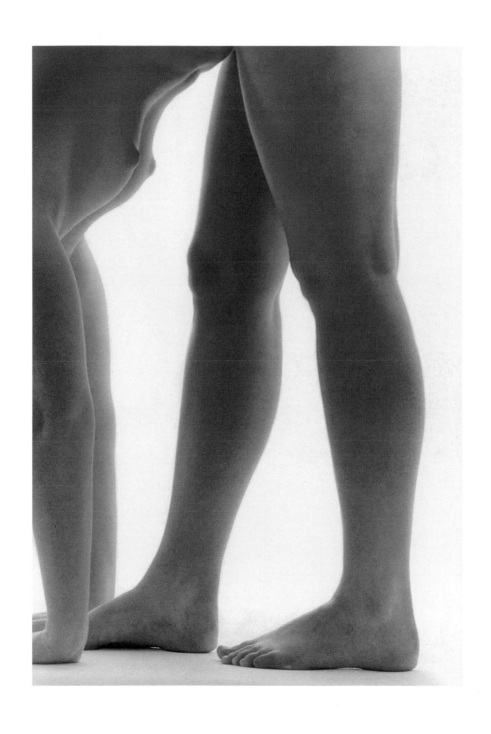

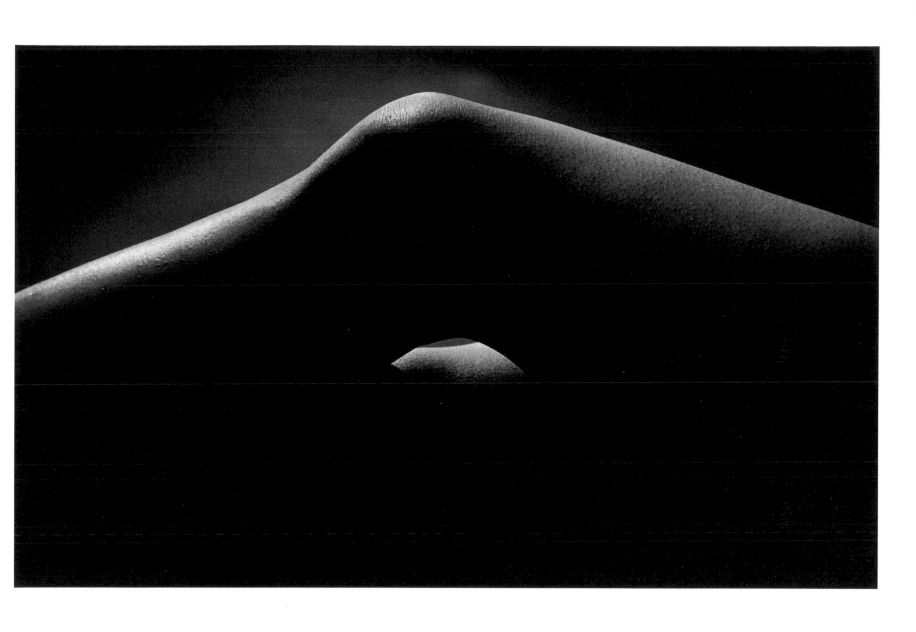

Mountain • 1983

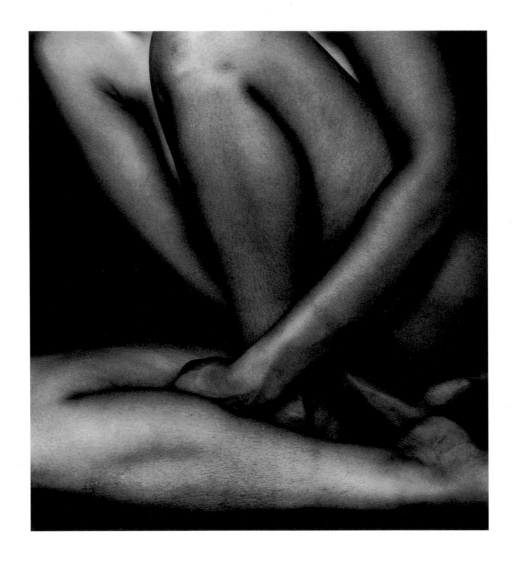

Crux • 1992

Leopard • 1989

Z-Form • 1983

Athena • 1990

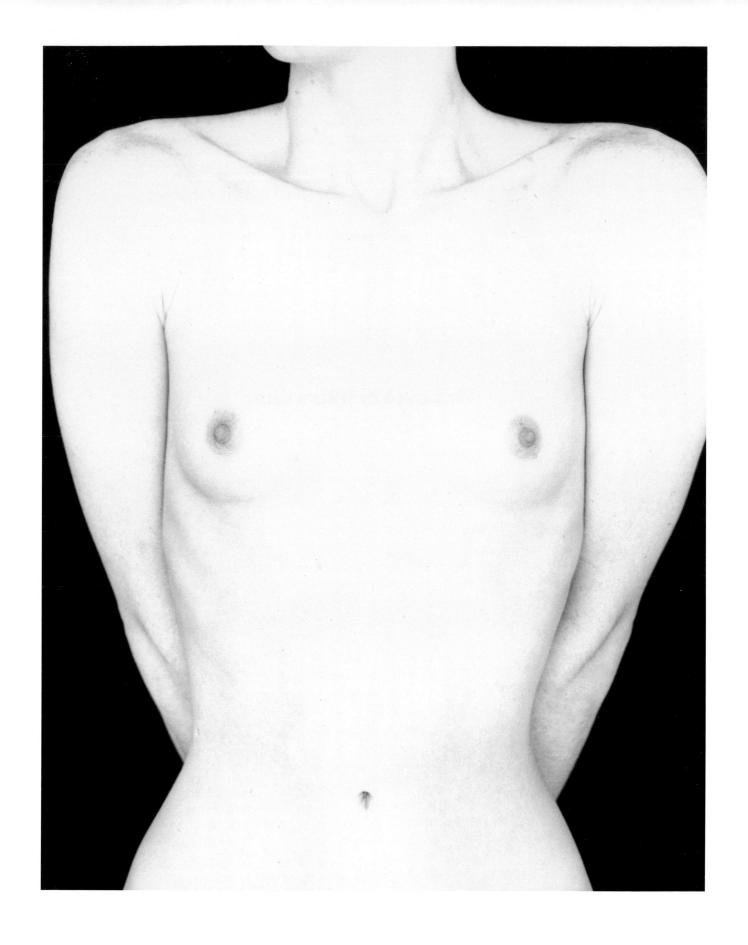

Urn • 1990

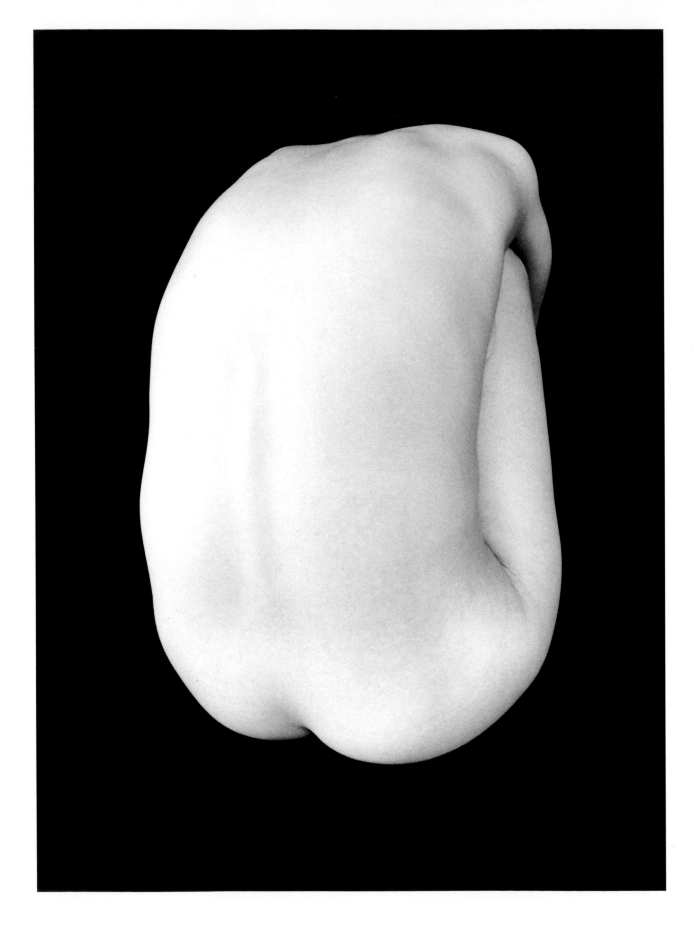

Pearl • 1990

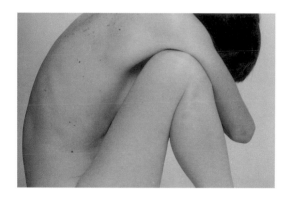

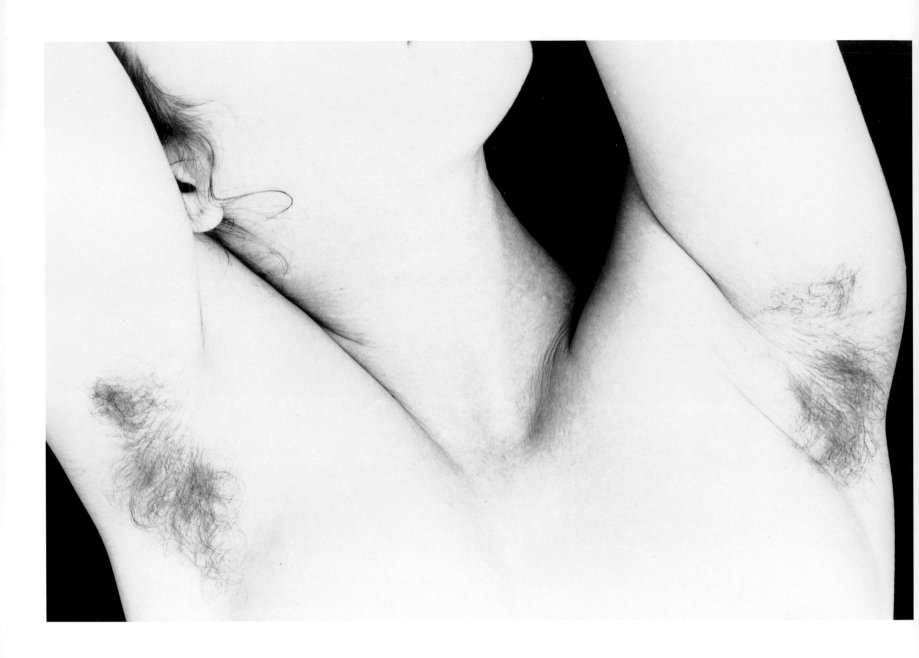

What Moved; What Was Still

One area of man's mind deals with present time, another with the future, another with the past. Traditional cultures pay more attention to the past, modern ones to the present and future. In Europe, during the Middle Ages, men gave highest priority to yet another area – the one that most interests me – that in which time plays no part.

Light is paint. Radiance and light are very close.

The irreducible magic of a great photograph is its radiance – its way of being translucent to the light which informs it from within. Great art can be likened to a Gothic cathedral, even if its proximate creator is an atheist.

Sculptor Henry Moore noted that 'In Greece the object seems to give off light as if it were lit up from inside itself.'

Pythagoras said: 'Limit gives form to the limitless.'

Poet/essayist Octavio Paz wrote: 'The Poem is a mask that hides the void.'

'He moves where you will never find his trace,' wrote Rilke. And again: 'Over and over by us torn in two, the god is the hidden place that heals again.'

Painter Paul Klee said: 'We are striving for the essence that hides behind the fortuitous.'

Matisse believed that 'The essential thing is to work in a state of mind that approaches prayer.'

Sculptor Constantine Brancusi said: 'It is not difficult to make things; what is difficult is to reach the state in which we can make them.'

Similarly Goethe: 'You understand the spirit to which you are equal.'

Thus photographer Alfred Stieglitz' advice to photographer Edward Weston: 'Treat anything you undertake with dignity.'

In the words of the Sanskrit Guru Gita: 'He moves and moves not; he is far as well as near, inside as well as outside everything.'

Another Sanskrit prayer, chanted in the mornings and evenings, reminds us that 'perfect comes from perfect.'

Meister Eckhart told his thirteenth century German congregation: 'The kind of work we do does not make us holy, but we may make it holy.'

A traditional Eastern Christian dictum has it that 'A man who prays only when he prays, is a man who does not pray at all.'

Aquinas wrote: 'Every form through which anything has existence is some kind of participation in the divine clarity.' And: 'Grace does not destroy nature, but completes it.'

Imbibing this medieval aesthetic on one level while forging radical modernism on another, James Joyce wrote: 'Aquinas says: *Ad pulcritudinem tria requiruntur, integritas consonantia, claritas.* I translate it so: *Three things are needed for beauty: wholeness, harmony and radiance.*'

The Upanishads – arguably the world's earliest scriptures – declare: 'By That Light, all this is illumined.'

The primacy of perception lies near the heart of many of the world's mystical traditions.

In common parlance: 'Seeing is believing.'

Novelist Doris Lessing, describing one of her strange and wild characters: 'He was everything he saw.'

A modern spiritual master, Muktananda, told his students: 'The world is as you see it.'

In this era of post-post-modernism, it's worth remembering T. S. Eliot's lines:

There is only the fight to recover what has been lost and found and lost again and again.

A most unfashionable way of thinking, these days. We need to tote our cameras back a thousand years.
In his book, *Medieval Civilization,* Jacques Le Goff writes:

What interested men in the Middle Ages was not what moved but what was still: Innovation was a sin: The hidden world was a sacred world: Nature was the great reservoir of symbols: Desiring to find behind the concrete, which was perceptible, the abstract, which was more real, and, on the other hand, trying to make this hidden reality appear in a form which could be perceived by the senses. Beauty was light: The first light was God.

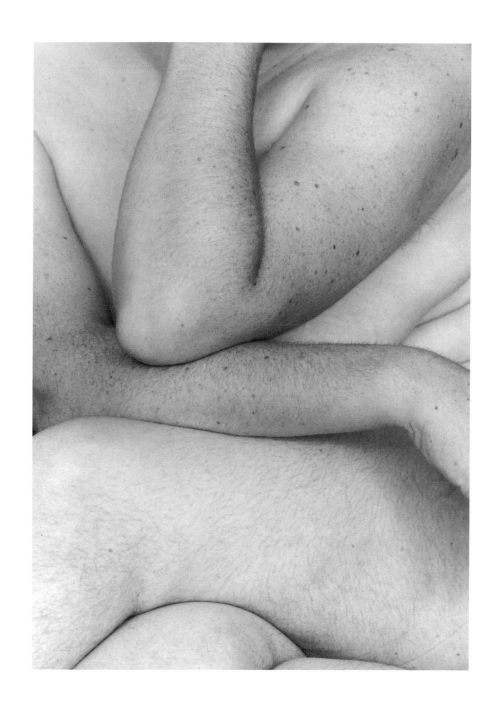

Confluence • 1992

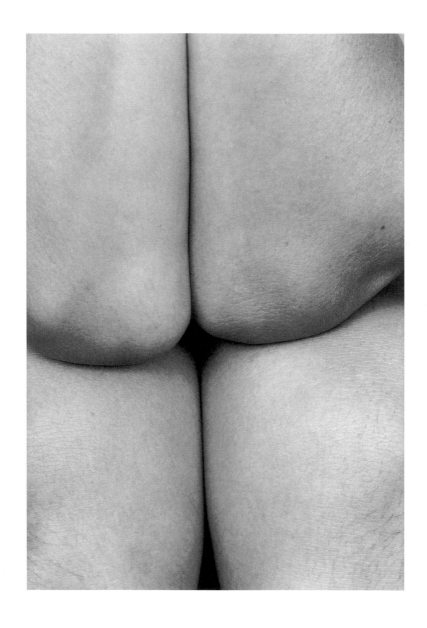

Prayer • 1992

Shakti • 1990

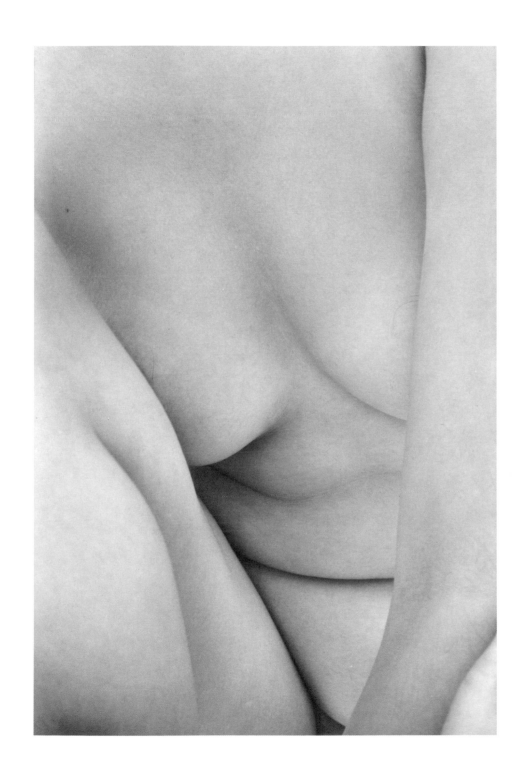

Brahmaputra • 1990

Willow • 1984

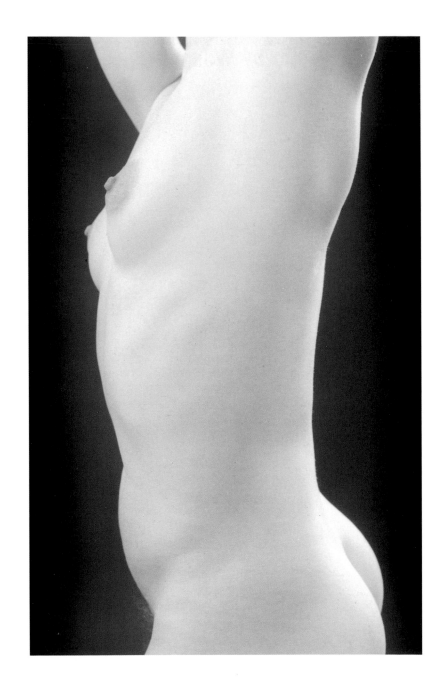

Alabaster • 1983

Homage • 1992

Seedling • 1990

Nudity and Knowing

Whoever knows himself is nude.

Nude because he lacks the clothing of false identity.

Perhaps he remains physically nude, like crazy people or like the disciples of St. Francis of Assisi.

Probably, however, he stays behind the mask of conformity in order to continue his assigned role in the theater of life.

While continuing to experience pain and joy, he maintains a kind of subtle, permanent delight underneath.

This experience may well remain hidden.

Perhaps the man who knows himself wears the mask of normalcy precisely because of his awareness of being nude.

He sees, at the same time, the nudity of everyone else – in their pain, in their eyes.

He treats them with tenderness.

Sight • 1995

Remember • 1990

Mystery • 1990

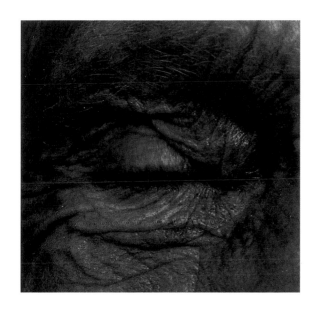

Dusk • 1992

Moment • 1993

Appearance • 1983

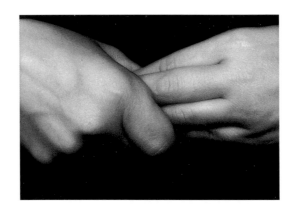

Suggestion • 1994

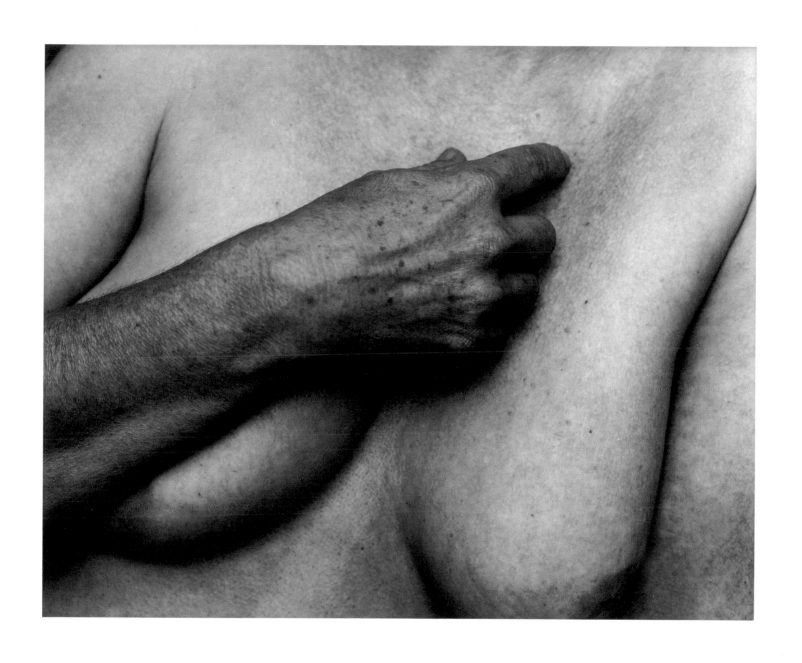

Char • 1992

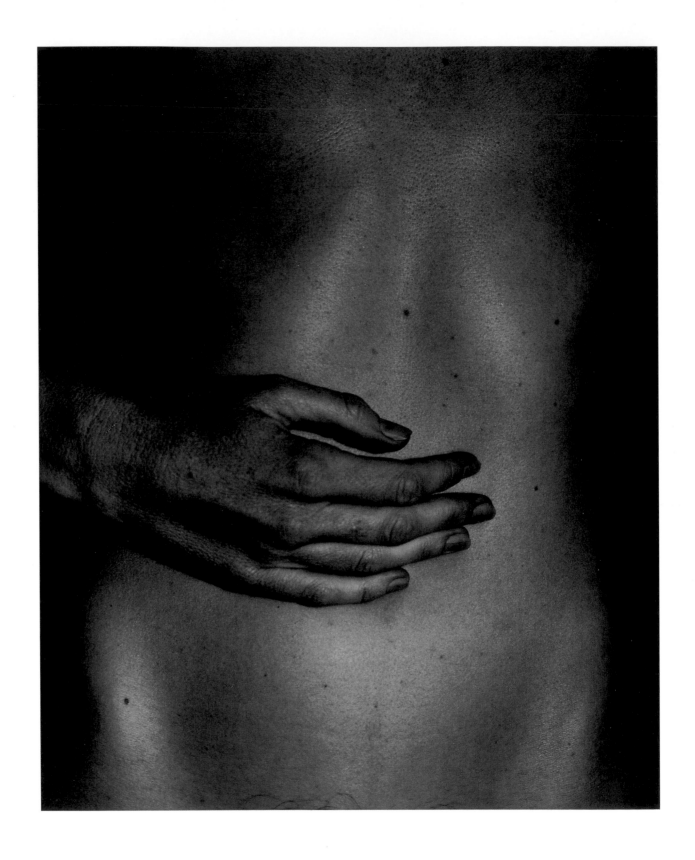

Intimation • 1991

Where the Poetry Comes From

Portraying the body – like all attempts to represent nature – is elusive and mysterious. To place a frame upon space and time is to limit the limitless. Nature herself does the same: a single object, such as a human body, is an expression, in concrete form, of the infinite, which is beyond form. The aim of art is to point back the other way – to express the mystery lying past the edges of the form. For this to happen, those edges are essential. The individual work of art is distinguished by its edges, just as bodies and other natural forms are.

The form can be stretched or reduced – i.e. to include relationships between bodies, or to focus on only one portion of a body. But the edges have to be there, at least by implication. They are the foundation of form.

To remove the boundaries between art and non-art, as some have tried to do, is to destroy art. There is nothing 'wrong' with vague, undefined, limitless sorts of happenings; but they will never achieve the aim of art, because they are unable to point beyond themselves. Nothing can point beyond itself if it has no edge where itself leaves off. In this sense Goethe's definition of a symbol is a definition of any true work of art:
It expresses itself fully, and points beyond itself.

Our minds are not made to grasp the infinite without the intervention of forms. Mystics able to see the One in its entirety are struck dumb, call it 'ineffable,' or speak in deceptively simple stories or metaphors.

Form and boundaries are a necessary but not sufficient condition of art. Thousands of rectangular snapshots roll out of minilabs every hour, all over the world. A work of art begins with those same four edges, but plays them so that, in Duke Ellington's words, it leaps 'beyond category.'

Every playing field – in sports or music, computer screens or the days and months of the year – has a frame around it. In each mundane event the universal force is veiled, but manifest. In our hurried, preoccupied lives we frequently find that it takes a special celebration, or some radical discontinuity, such as death, to jar our awareness back to ultimate things – to restore our sense of awe. Fine art, to be worthy of the name, does this.

Such, at least, is my aesthetic standard. If any of my pictures approach it, they are informed, not by me, but by the streams of cultures that fed me: by those who helped me to see.

As photographer W. Eugene Smith said: 'I learned it all from Beethoven.'

Can it be an accident that so many photographers have had an interest in music? The 'subject' is not it. Propagandistic photographs, carrying some message about events, can roughly be compared to programmatic music. There is nothing 'wrong' with either, in themselves; indeed, it would be folly to suppose that social concerns, or religious mythologies, or the many functional uses of music, have not been springboards for works of towering genius in every medium.

But what unites these works is not their programs or uses or ideological references, mostly quite localized, but their masterly manipulation, within the given frame, of the non-referential elements particular to that art.

The emotional variety and profundity of Beethoven's great works flow from his handling of purely musical elements, not from the ideologies of his day. His alternating sections of compressed or expanded space, his startling tensions and gentle releases, his overarching momentum from launch to arrival – such internal dynamics, within the conventional movements, can be compared to the spacial, linear, textural and tonal relationships within the four edges of the best pictures by Gustav Le Gray or Henri Cartier-Bresson, Alfred Stieglitz or Paul Strand, Edward Weston or Olivia Parker, Nicholas Nixon or Sally Mann.

The mysterious core of aesthetics is how these abstract internal dynamics, played against the bounding edges of the form, seem, when masterfully handled, to spring from the inner harmonies of life itself. At this point, poetry and spirituality become one.

Representations of the human form issue from many levels of seeing – worshipful to trivial. As the *Bhagavad Gita* reminds us, the body is a field, available for planting any way we choose. Photographers have utilized the nude in innumerable ways, virtually since the invention of the camera. Of most lasting value have been those pictures which, through masterful use of the elements inherent in the medium, evoke the spiritual poetry inherent in ourselves.

Praise • 1990

Descent • 1989

My Concerns

One reason I concern myself with the nude is that I am concerned with universals. Clothing is specific to time, place, culture; the body is not.

I work within the broad tradition of the nude in western art, not so much thematically as formally. I attend to such things as precise framing; negative spaces; relationships of line, volume and tone.

I strive for Aquinas' 'wholeness, harmony, and radiance.' A work with these qualities, whatever its content, reflects the spiritual order of the universe.

Dunes • 1984

Coincidence • 1990

Victoria • 1990

Earthform • 1989

Recumbent • 1989

Maillol • 1983

In Praise of Polarity

We live between poles. The union of seeming opposites is a mark of high illumination, high art. This cannot be bought cheaply. The polarity has to be felt. The tension of the trial, the pain of the flaying, must precede the glory of the resurrection.

Austerity and eros, the celestial and the vulgar, Apollo and Adam, the permanent and the momentary, geometry and the tactile, stone and breath, the straightedge and the curve, the ideal and the imperfect: within these crossing fields of force, the tradition of the nude in Western art finds its dynamic existence.

This is as true for current photographs by Lee Friedlander as for the ancient sculptures of Praxiteles.

Sir Kenneth Clark writes: 'Of all Raphael's marvellous gifts, that which was most completely his own, and seems to come from the radiant center of his personality, was his power of grasping the ideal through the senses.'

Clark goes on to remind us that the highly sensual Rubens was also the leading religious painter of his time. His nudes are 'both responsive and detached...grateful for life, and their gratitude spreads all through their bodies...in his spendidly unified character, sensuality could not be dissociated from praise.'

Influence • 1993

Cascade • 1993

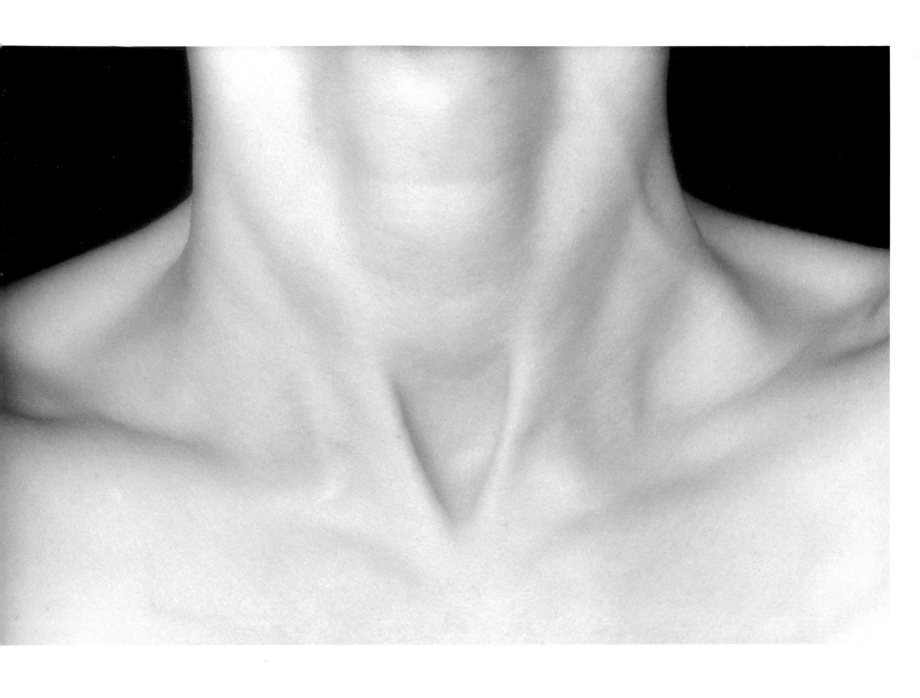

Temple • 1994

From my Notebooks

The highest use of nudity in art is not nudity *per se*, but as a shorthand for the whole person. The whole person, in turn, is a shorthand for all that is.

Attitude is everything. Giotto's clothed Biblical figures are more naked than any image in the skin magazines.

As with other arts, the depiction of the nude is inevitably a depiction of the inner condition of the artist. What a picture means is also a depiction of the viewer.

——————

Scientists commonly talk of space curving back on itself; of the impossibility of specifying exactly where anything is; of singularities in the universe.

Why, then, do we continue, mechanistically, in picturing progress as linear? Why not jump off the one-dimensional time-line?

The idea of revolving adds a dimension to that of merely evolving. Making a revolution means coming full circle.

Progress could be pictured as a kind of spiral staircase, evolving in one dimension while revolving in the other.

——————

If one really wished to upset (read: be ignored by) the pundits of the present, one would write an autobiography entitled, 'Confessions of an Unrepentant Eternalist.' Public utterance of such thoughts has become as taboo as talking of sex once was.

——————

Einstein said: 'Few there are that see with their own eyes and feel with their own heart.'

The most important photographs of the twentieth century may well be those taken of – and from – outer space. Aside from the scientific benefits, this trove of material helps restore some of the longer perspectives which have tended to be eroded, in our time, by the welter of the everyday.

———————

Differences in the qualities of light affect different skins differently, in turn affecting different films and papers differently. Try to learn a little more about this each day.

———————

'This is an organized mass of light and energy,' said Dr. Jeffrey R. Kuhn, an astronomer at Michigan State University…'Since it's a smooth distribution, the outer part really is connected to the inner part. It's a very large, organized galaxy.'

The astronomers said the density, luminosity and smoothness of the large galaxy were possible clues to its formation and to the nature of invisible matter – dark matter of the missing mass – that makes up most of the universe.

– JOHN NOBLE WILFORD,
  'Largest Galaxy Found,' *The New York Times, October 26, 1990*

———————

One of my favorite recent bits of critical writing was the blanket dismissal of whole categories of photographic subject matter, regardless of treatment, because those subjects had already been 'fully explored'! At that rate art in general has a short future.

Nothing worthwhile is ever safely dead. Someone will always gleefully blast the lid off the coffin.

Photography of the nude celebrates the meeting of the most elemental thing in the universe – light – with the most highly evolved thing – the human body.

'Perhaps, after all, ugliness may have a useful qualifying effect on sweetness and affection; at present it is itself one of the worst affectations of the century.'

HENRY PEACH ROBINSON (1869)

'My husband from first to last has watched every picture with delight, and it is my daily habit to run to him with every glass upon which a fresh glory is newly stamped, and listen to his enthusiastic applause.

'This habit of running into the dining-room with my wet pictures has stained an immense quantity of table linen with nitrate of silver, indelible stains, that should have been banished from any less indulgent household.'

JULIA MARGARET CAMERON (1874)

'I would rather have ten people who understand and appreciate my work, than ten thousand who get excited because they're told it's the thing to do.'

BRETT WESTON (1992)

'We are all students.'

PAUL STRAND

Pornography is depressing – *dispiriting* – because it splits off one part of our being from the rest. Whether a picture or story is pornographic has less to do with subject matter than with the intention, the tone, of both author and consumer. Raw or sophisticated, pornography can be recognized by narrowness of intention, a shrinking of ourselves – because it leaves out love.

'The Naked One of blackest hue
Lights the Lotus of the Heart.'

SONG OF KALI

———————

'The Self that hovers in between is neither man nor woman.'

DASIMAYYA

———————

'You can confiscate money in hand:
can you confiscate the body's glory?
Or peel away every strip you wear,
but can you peel away
the Nothing, the Nakedness
that covers and veils?
To the shameless girl
wearing the
White Jasmine Lord's
light of morning
you fool:
where's the need
for cover and jewel?'

MAHAHEVIYAKKA

———————

'Thou art woman. Thou art man. Thou art the youth and also the maiden…
Thou art the seasons and the seas.'

UPANISHADS

Imogen • 1982

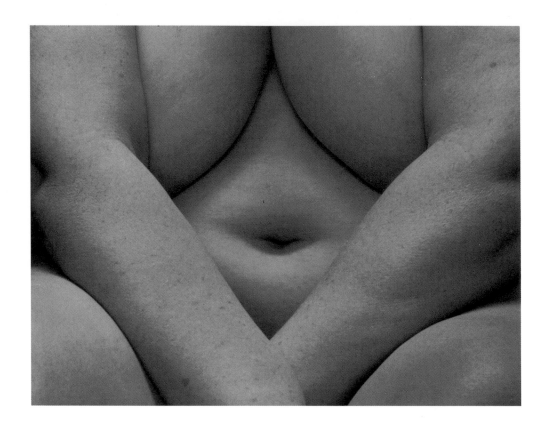

Quilt • 1989

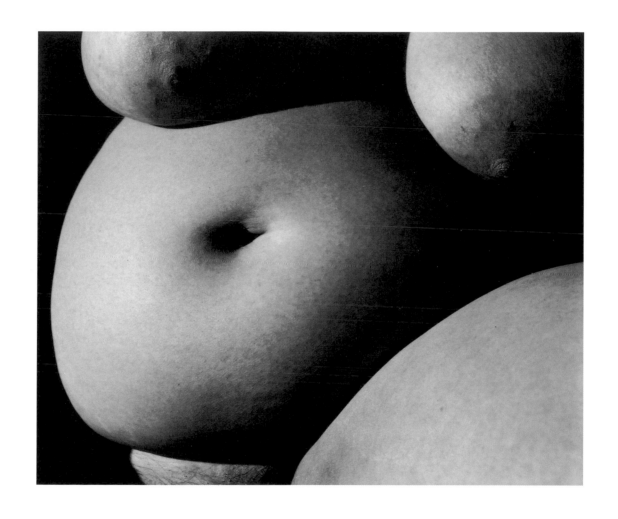

Melones • 1989

Truth in art is the unity of a thing with itself:
the outward rendered expressive of the inward:
the soul made incarnate:
the body instinct with spirit.

OSCAR WILDE